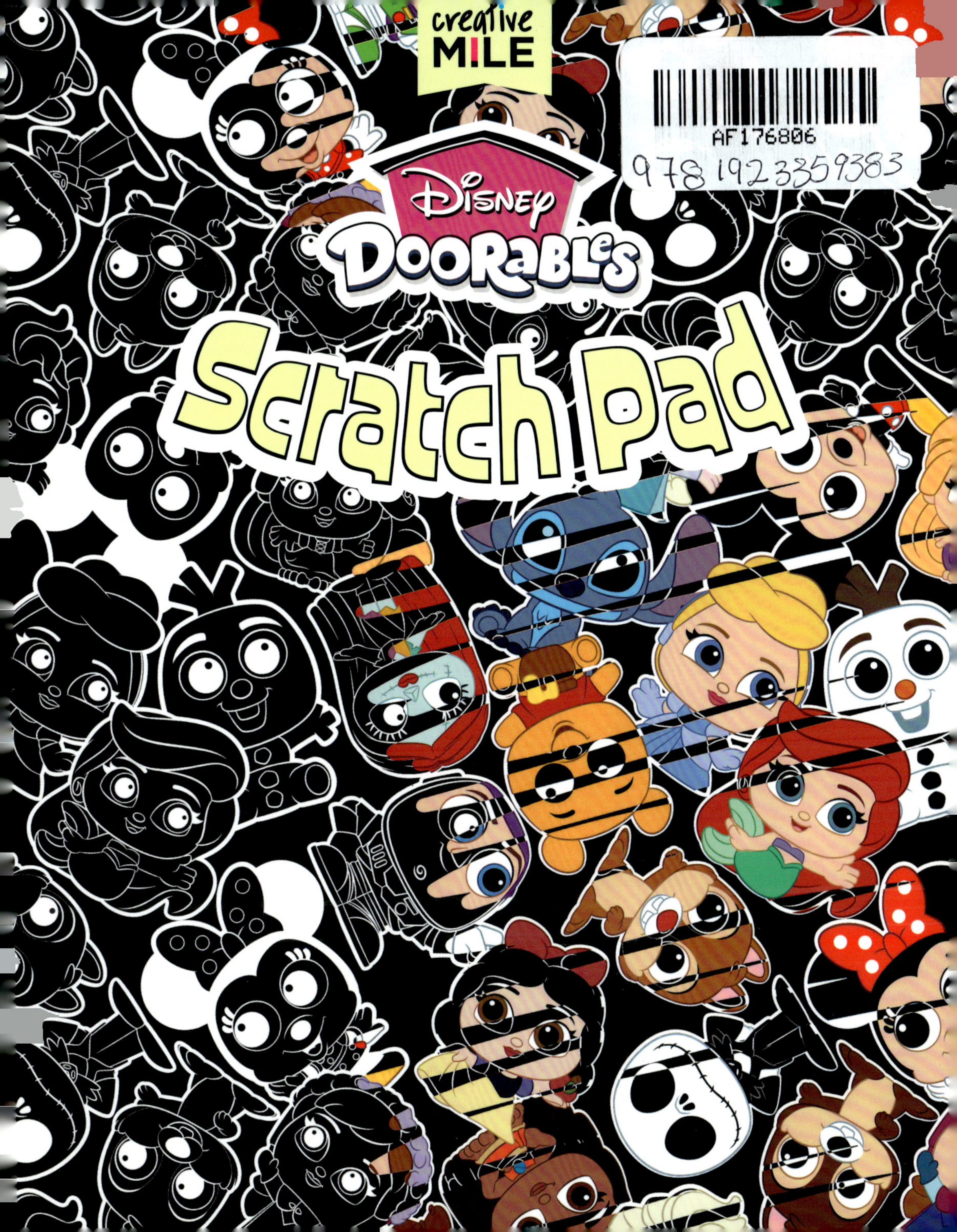
creative
MILE
Disney
Doorables
Scratch Pad

©Disney

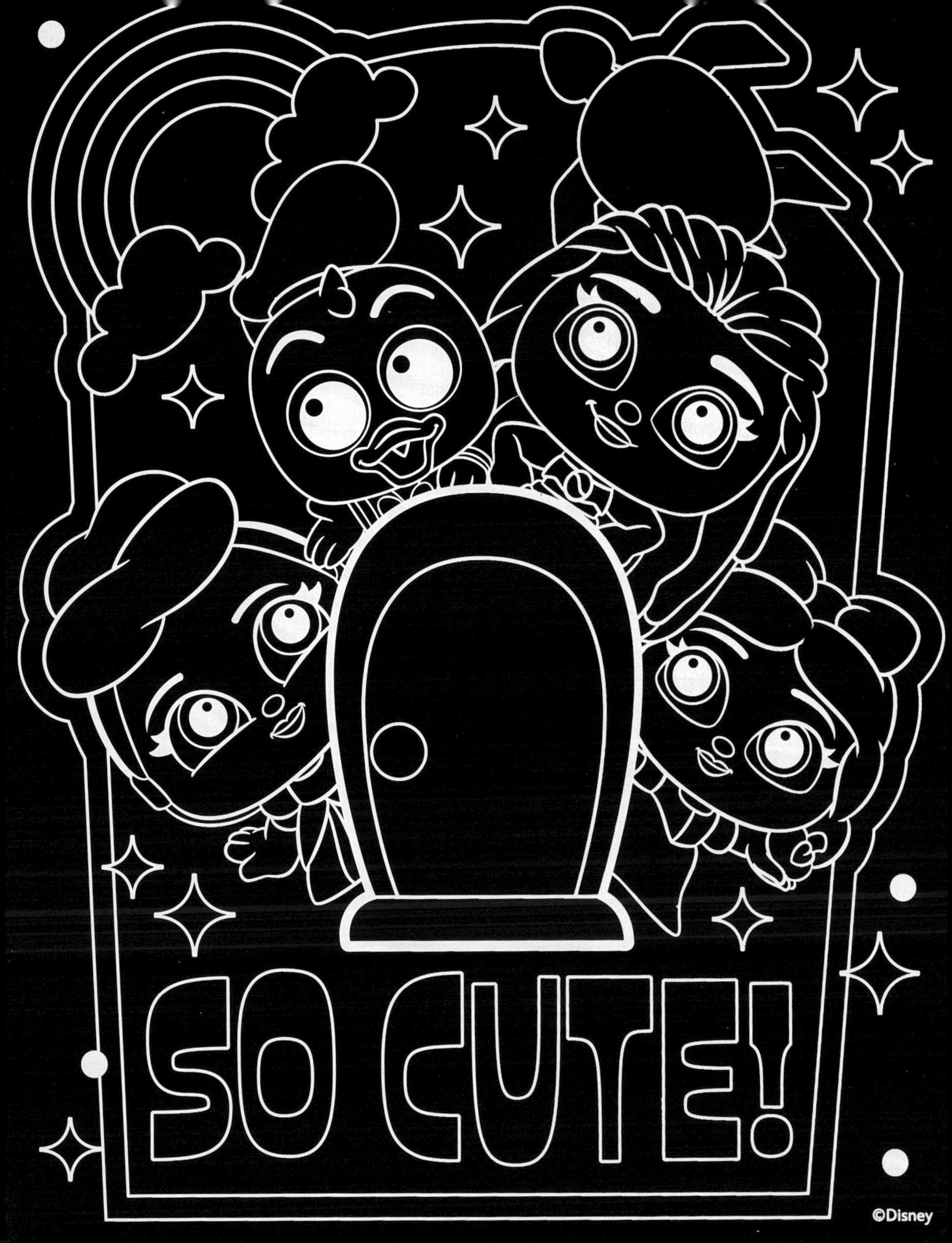
SO CUTE!
©Disney

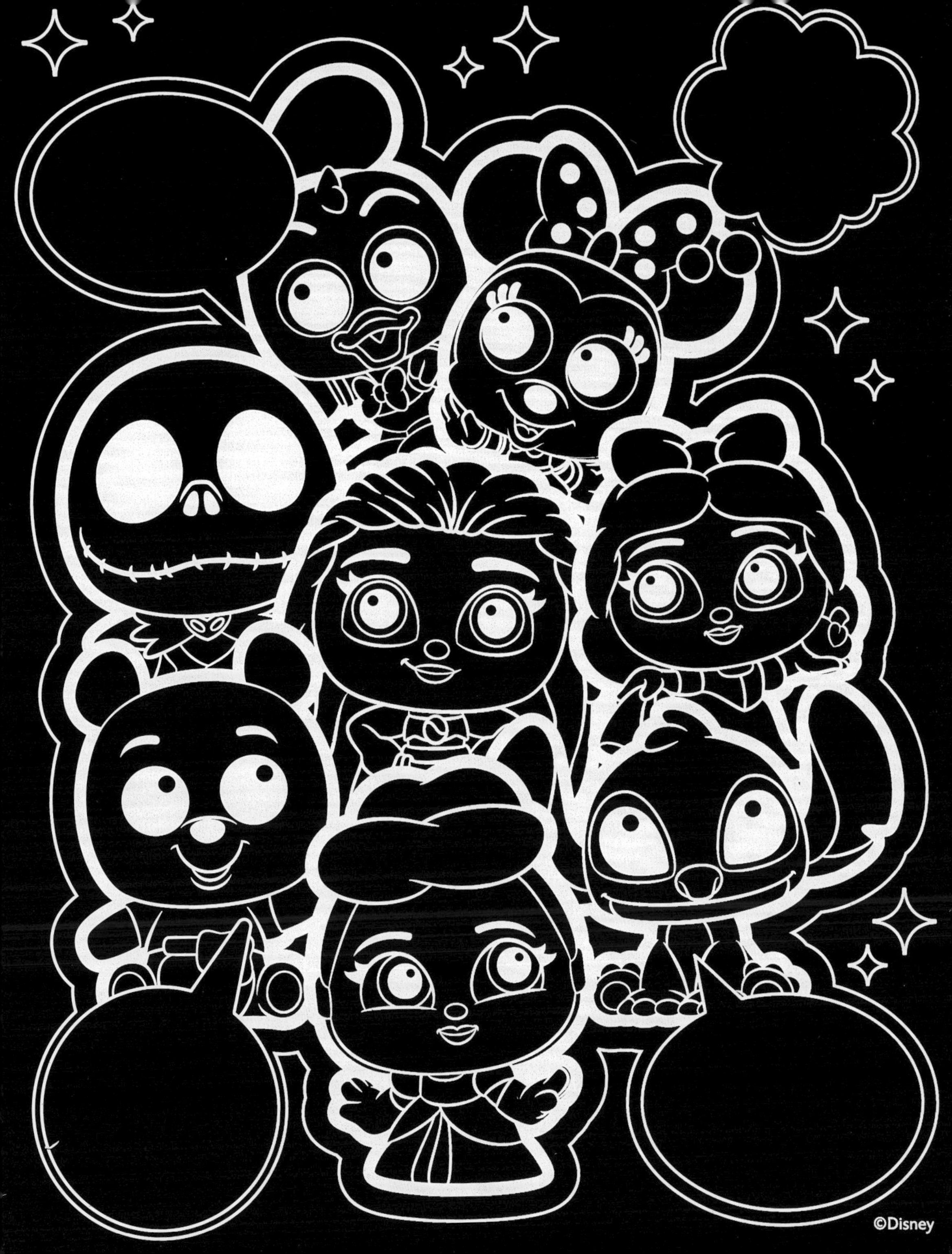

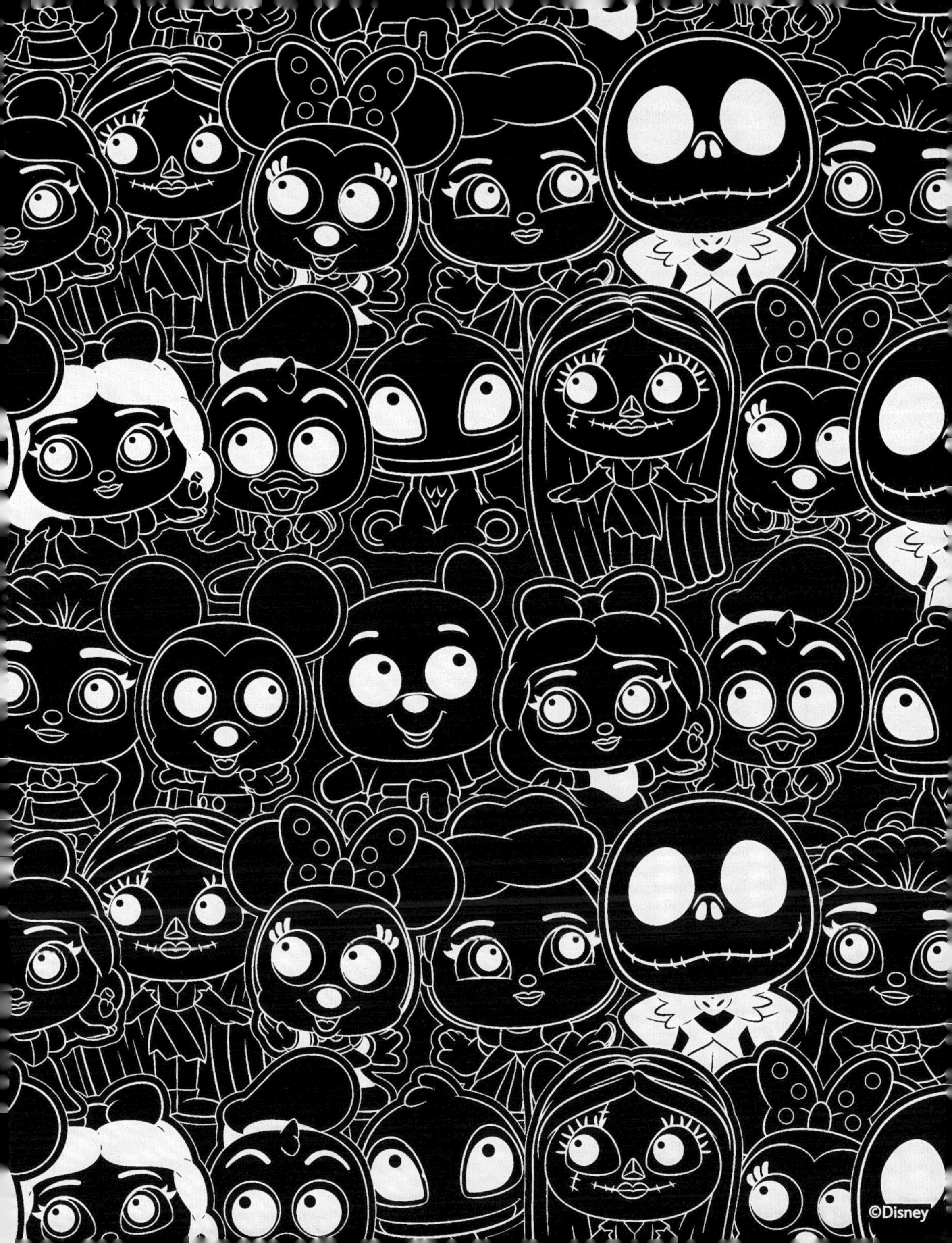

VIBES
BESTIE
SQUAD GOALS
GOOD

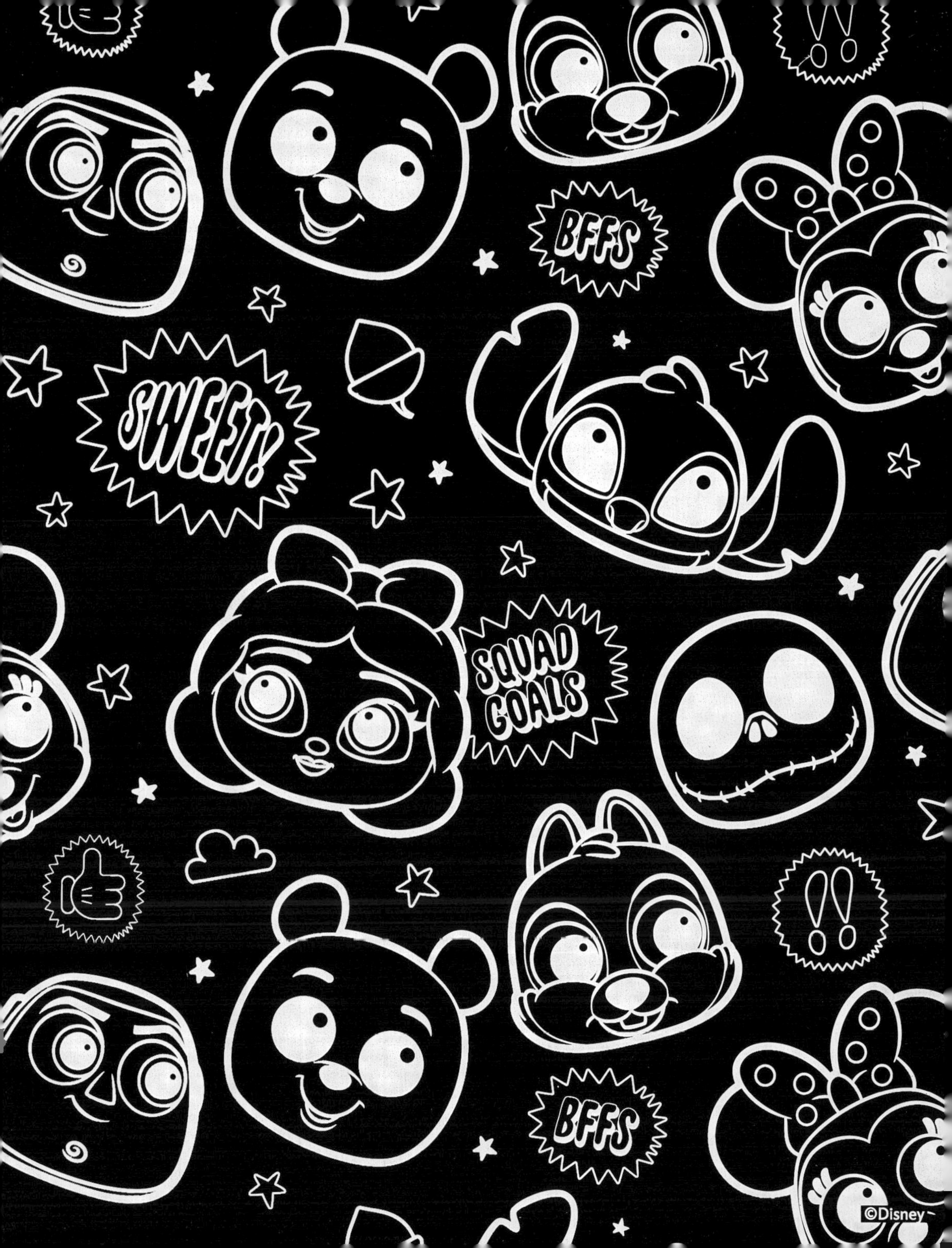
BFFS
SWEET!
SQUAD GOALS
BFFS
©Disney

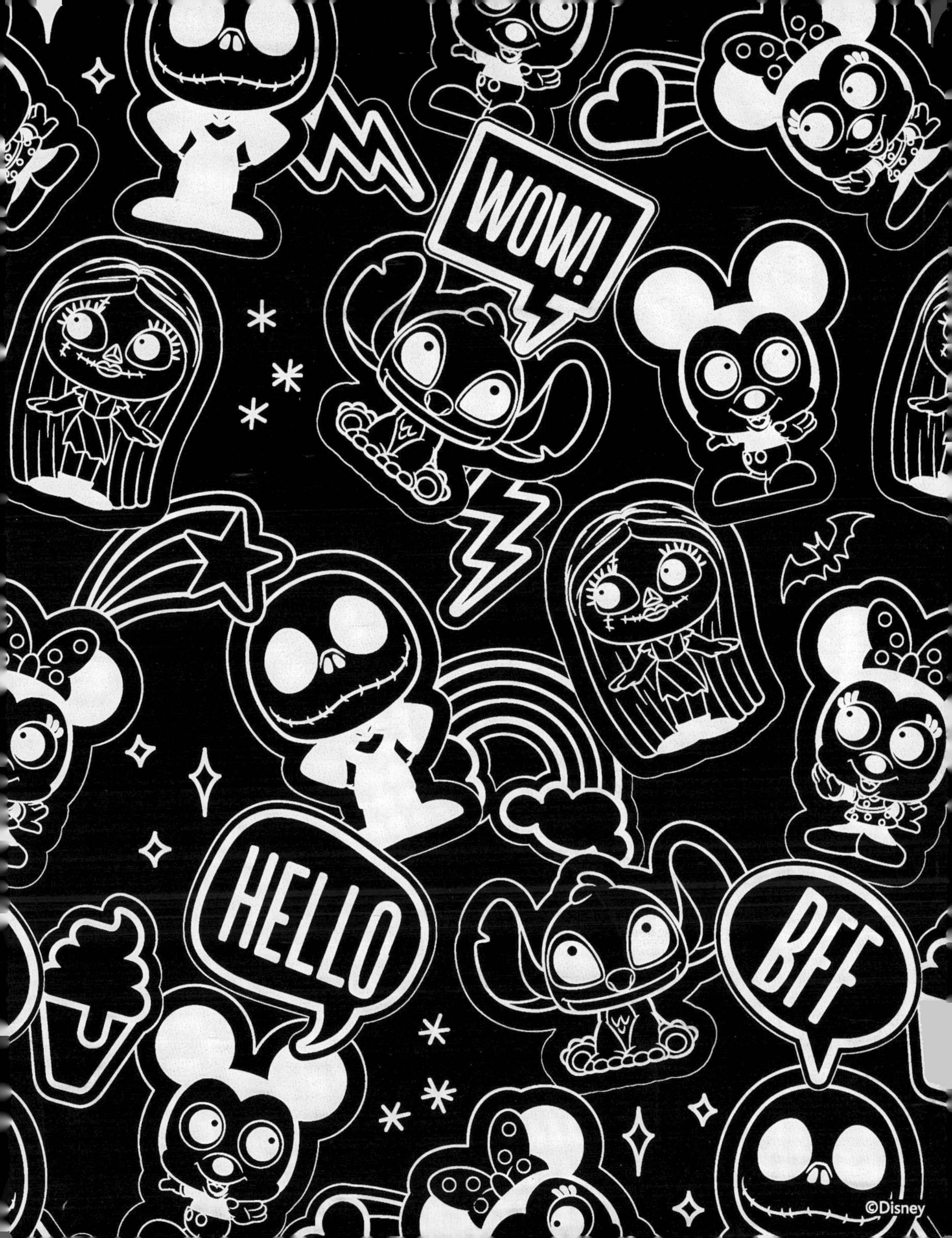
WOW!
HELLO
BFF
©Disney